WomensWords

Women Today

Edited by

Liz Wakefield

First published in Great Britain in 1997 by
WOMENSWORDS
1-2 Wainman Road, Woodston,
Peterborough, PE2 7BU
Telephone (01733) 230746
Fax (01733) 230751

HB ISBN 1 86188 772 8
SB ISBN 1 86188 777 9

FOREWORD

Although we are a nation of poetry writers we are accused of not reading poetry and not buying poetry books: after many years of listening to the incessant gripes of poetry publishers, I can only assume that the books they publish, in general, are books that most people do not want to read.

Poetry should not be obscure, introverted, and as cryptic as a crossword puzzle: it is the poet's duty to reach out and embrace the world.

The world owes the poet nothing and we should not be expected to dig and delve into a rambling discourse searching for some inner meaning.

The reason we write poetry (and almost all of us do) is because we want to communicate: an ideal; an idea; or a specific feeling. Poetry is as essential in communication, as a letter; a radio; a telephone, and the main criteria for selecting the poems in this anthology is very simple: they communicate.

For many years the most influential poets have been males and it's only in recent years have we accepted that there are many female poets who are just as talented!

People often suggest that in the past there were few women poets, but in actual fact there were but poetry was merely a hobby after dealing with the home and family. Many females kept their poems to themselves for various reasons, possibly for fear of being ridiculed or because they felt guilty for spending time enjoying themselves.

But today there are more and more female poets who are open and proud about their poetry. They're not out to prove they are better poets but to show they too can write poetry of a high standard.

This anthology brings together a selection of today's up and coming female poets. All the poems are original and innovative giving the reader an insight into their lives, the issues which are close to their hearts and the subjects which inspire their poetry.

CONTENTS

Work

I'm not a go-getter my needs are simple and few
so why do I feel under pressure in everything I do
It's targets this objectives that -
Personal Review & Development? - I'm a failure
'Cause I'm happy where I'm at!
I'm a 90s woman let me make that quite clear
But I mean 1890s wrong century I fear!

J Fitzsimmons

Memories

A rainbow arching the sky
flashes of lightning rumbles of thunder
a black velvet sky and a silver crescent moon
sunlight sparkling on water
the aroma of fresh baked bread
and newly mown grass
the freshness after the rain
swans gliding on a pond
coloured butterflies flitting to and fro
the sounds of bumble bees buzzing
walking through the woods
bracken beneath one's feet
gathering rich brown chestnuts
seeing bluebells, white snowdrops
and pale yellow primroses
a field full of red poppies
yellow buttercups, orange marigolds
pale blue linseed bright yellow mustard
and oxeye daisies
avenues of trees with pink and white cherry blossom
gathering teasels to brush one's hair
then feeding donkeys apples
their muzzles gentle against my skin.

Lyn Chambers

Sunny Days

What's going to become of us. The world is in a mess.
They have taken away our joy of life, and all our happiness.
Our children should be safe and sound to play out in the sun,
To play with their bikes and skipping ropes and hop and laugh and run.

A mugging a bag-snatch, the world's full of crime.
I know what I'd do to them if they were mine.
But justice says help them as they haven't got much.
But I never had lots but knew not to touch.

Things that were others, others not mine.
But it did not make me have a lifetime of crime.
So stop being so kind to bad people today.
Then once more in the sunshine our children can play.

C E Branton

WOMAN OF DEED

Don't ever underestimate a woman
Good in this world women do.
In changes over years they have adapted
Or caused changes to be made for better
Achieve a lot for others through caring
A woman's touch at much of life is not just a point of view.
Many a modern time woman hold key jobs in working life.
Combined with running homes minding children
A very difficult task for many
But paying your way in this day this age
To get cash to cope with cost of living
Many women go to work to help out financially
Help their men folk supportive of one another
Keeping life in perspective which is very nice.

Victoria Joan Theedam

One Woman's Word Against The Trend

When I was young, I thought I was
A liberated woman.
My mother was, a pioneer in every way
And broke many a rule of her day.
Did many things against the code,
Drove all kinds of vehicles on the road.
Nursed wounded soldiers amidst shocking sights
And always fought for a woman's right.
To do the things which custom said
Would bring down scorn upon her head.

But, through it all, she admired men
And gave credit generously to them, when
They were strong and brave; and overcame
Their initial shock when she proved the same!
Today's women, I find, are not like her
And seem to me, to have lost all round,
For feminists use ugly words and sound
So unlikeable.

Surely men and women need not divide
And in coarsened speech each other deride?
For me, I have no desire
To fight in battles in war or peace
And wish this sniping shrill would cease;
And though I defend my right to be
No man's doormat, I still can see
Male virtues, values, in society.

I tell my daughter, the golden rule
Is, respect yourself and you will find
No need to bluster and leave behind
The finer things which women can give
Even to this modern world in which we live.
Dirty jokes and blasphemy do not prove your superiority;
Quite the opposite s true and, *modern woman*, it's up to *you.*

Deirdre White

UNTITLED

The woman of the nineties
has come a long, long way
from her counter part of the 50s
who had few roles to portray.

Back then she was a lover a wife and a mum of a few,
a labourer in her own home with monotonous tasks to pursue.
A bringer-up of children whilst doing household chores;
this was the daily grind of women then, with limited open doors.

Many doors have opened now and women have seen the light,
they are capable achievers and have learnt to be forthright.
A woman of the nineties sets out and follows her goals
and is now an avid juggler of several varied roles.

The aroma from the fairer sex,
can be found in the executive suite.
And now her head is held up high
as she has become one of the elite.

From DIY to earning a wage
today's woman is known to adapt
a different life from her mother's
which was very matter of fact.

M Buckley

Don't Cry Ailsa

If you have a sister
Treat her with respect
Don't let silly arguments
Put you to the test
I fell out with Ailsa
And caused her lots of stress
And I was too pigheaded
To know I made a mess
When she came to see me
Her heart was broke in two
She wasn't thinking of herself
She just said 'I love you,'
And though the row was settled
And she left my house in peace
I was riddled with shame and guilt
For the way I made her feel
Life's too short for heartaches
It should be filled with love
And I dearly love my sister
As sure as God's above.

Corinne Tuck

Try To Smile

I watch the world go by
with clouds of smoke before my face
as people pass I wonder if
they too feel out of place

Does everybody know just why
they're here, what to believe
or do they feel as I do now
that they never will achieve

The world is strange, the people too
am I the same as them
will we ever know what each wants
will we ever think the same

If each of us can try to smile
say hi, give helping hands
perhaps we can fulfil our dreams
and succeed in God's great plan.

Carolyn R Cunningham

The Voice Of The Unborn Child

Six weeks have slipped by, and still you don't know
That safe, and secure within your womb I have begun to grow
My looks, and personality have been formed already
I am a little bit like you mum, and a whole lot like my daddy.

Eight weeks have passed, and now you know I'm here,
I can sense your mixed emotions, and recognise your fear.
I hate it when each morning, I make you feel so ill,
And all the while you have not told, my daddy about me still.

Twelve weeks have gone by, soon everyone will know
I will change your life forever, as each day you watch me grow
But I promise you, that beyond these tears, there will be so much joy
And secretly you're wondering, if I'm a girl or boy.

Sixteen weeks have passed, and I'm so aware of every move you make
You are fighting with your conscience every step you take
Your heartbeat is so comforting right next to my own
By now you can feel me moving, you shouldn't feel alone.

Twenty-four weeks is here now, I know today is the day
My hearing is so good, and how I hear you pray
It doesn't really matter mum, we can make it on our own
Thank you for allowing me the chance to be born.

Anne Eves

HAPPY DAYS

My Granny's little cottage gleamed all through and through
The old black grate just glistened - the brass and copper too
Her oak Welsh dresser looked a treat with pretty china on it
Her mother's picture on the wall - in her Sunday bonnet
Gran's smile would welcome me she'd give me such a hug
The memory of it still gives my heart a tug
A clean cloth on the table everything so neat
But - there was always silence when we sat down to eat

Her washing on the clothes-line was always snowy white
Her dolly tub and mangle always served her right
She hated new contraptions was suspicious of them all
Always time to stop and chat whenever I would call
I loved it when she lit the lamps - into the fire I'd stare
Imagine pictures in the flames I felt contented there

Grans today are busy they may hold down a job
Not for them drab black clothes and kettle on the hob
They wear the latest fashions and whatever hair's in style
No hair held up with combs and pins and fashioned in a pile
They own the latest gadgets to help them run their home
Whenever things are faulty they're on the telephone

No old tin baths before the fire and down the garden loos
They've all mod cons with shower and bath and use whiche'er
they choose
How the world has altered - values too may change
The times I knew have long since gone -
But memories remain.

Corrie Wright

Mid-Life Crisis

I thought you wanted me for love
But that was not the truth
You hit a mid-life crisis
and you were clutching at your youth.

Lesley Jane Gammon

A Woman's Lament

Oh give me a man that is 'new'.
The sort that knows housework's for two.
He'd work equal shares, up and downstairs,
And takes turns at cleaning the loo.

He wouldn't need to be handsome,
Or strong like Delilah's Samson.
I know I could lust for a man who would dust.
To me he'd be worth a king's ransom.

I'd cheer when he expertly hoovered,
As tables and chairs he manoeuvered.
When I called, 'Coffee's up,' he'd pour me a cup
And then clean the blind that is louvered.

A new man would instantly please
If he chose to defrost the deep-freeze.
A regular sorter of all that water
Would make me go weak at the knees.

With energy saved on the cleaning
I'd be swinging downtown in the evening,
At a trendy new pub or a late night-club
That normally I wouldn't be seen in.

But if your man, like mine, isn't 'new'.
There's not a lot you can do.
If you love him, then stay. If not, get away.
And then maybe your dream will come true.

Elizabeth Opie

MALE ORDER

Square tiled wall running through the length
Of a cold blue hall,
We follow your line to the frosted door
And fall onto slabbed chill pavement,
Where winter thought half kept
On cracked paving stones
Ice swept and male blown
Freezes our humanity from the bone
Into frigid shapes
Demanded by the male elite,
And as ice-chains close
Around our freedom,
Locking mind and feet in an ice sheet
In iceberg pain we find
Ourselves living within the links
Of lost liberty.

Pat Isiorho

Betrayal

As you sip your coffee, a friend I thought in my home,
I can't wait for the moment when you leave and are gone.
Out of my company, my house, my sight
For you say you love my husband - but I will fight.
I dread the moment when I'm alone in bed
Now you've confessed, anymore to be said?
Does he tell you he loves you, his thoughts, his ideas?
Whispered dreams and ambitions along with his fears.
With him I have travelled life's troubled miles,
Through the anguish and anxieties, I long for his smile,
Supporting me, helping me to ride our storms and bad weather
Never doubting that love would keep us together.
But now you've returned, an old flame from the past
Hoping this time his feelings will last.
Praising him, flattering him, hanging on to his every word.
Telling him he looks fantastic when we know he looks absurd
In his Versace jeans and waistcoat to match,
Wearing a hideous toupeé, sporting a greying moustache,
You only want his money, his company and his shares.
Greed is your only partner, you don't really care.
So please, leave us alone to continue our lives.
You will never have him, for I am his wife.

Josephine Burnett

Lonely

Lonely sits the rain-drenched steps
while children call her names,
She hides away in her inner self
ignoring their childish games.
She tugs at the hood of her worn duffel coat
pours waters from the hole in her shoe,
Pulls a wet cloth from her pocket of tricks
and sneezes into dampness 'Aatchoo.'
Pretending the words do not hurt her
she rises and staggers away
her eyes are filled with tears
but abuse is a norm to her day.
The soup kitchen is open
she picks up her cup and her bowl,
A pastor holds her by the hand
and prays for Lonely's soul.
For a while she feels the warmth and company
hot tea and a bowl of soup,
Blending into people like her
here inside she is part of a group.
But too soon it is time to leave
back where cruelty rides,
Back to the squat of the homeless
the place where Lonely abides.
When the rain falls and cascades on the steps
spare a thought for Lonely,
All alone and bereft
on a path never smooth, but stony,
For she must have had her hopes and dreams
though none of them came true,
And I wonder if just one of them
was to be as fortunate as you.

Jacquie Williams

I'M GETTING MARRIED

Four years we've been together
I never thought the day would come
when you'd get down on your knee
and ask the blessing from my mum
'Will you marry me?' You ask
'Yes' is my only answer
I start arranging dates
for the year 2000 and ever after
long white dress
bluebells and lavender flowers
bridesmaids in blue
and I'll leave the best man to you
now I'm waiting for my perfect day
(well let's hope it will be)
when I'm standing at the altar
we're getting married you and me!

Natasha Mealing

WOMEN SHOULD STAND TOGETHER

For centuries we have been exploited and oppressed
Hidden in the background to tend to the nest,
Forced to live a life where we were controlled and used
Covered by their dominance and constantly abused.
Now we have laws which help reduce their force
We have the freedom to enter marriage and to divorce,
Domestic violence is acknowledged and social care is near,
Our experiences are so common now we don't have to live in fear.
Better education and training mean we can aim for a good occupation
Safer contraceptives enable us to control the population,
Women's rights are increasing and our power is now a threat
We can pursue everything we want, our opponents are already in debt.

Lisa Sheehan

SUDDEN DEATH

Don't leave me now, not at this time.
Because I am yours, and you are mine.
What will I do without your care?
What will I do if you're not there?
To take care of me in our own world
Our lives spent together; a history unfurled.
Of worry and care through war, and then peace.
Buying a car or having a lease.
Caring for childen, through thick or thin
Facing the battle, to finally win.
So don't leave me now not at this time.
I'm so lost without you, because you are mine.

Jennifer A Hawkins

ME

My name is . . .

Take my hand
And meet my gaze;
Then
Talk a while;
Make me smile.
Get to know me.

My name is . . .

Hear my voice
And see my face;
But,
Don't try to change
Or rearrange.
Just let me be.

Shaped by life and parents' hands,
I'm not my brother,
Nor my sister;
Not a clone;
I stand alone;
For I am *me*.

My name is . . .
Joan.

Joan Ashwell

DEAR EMILY PANKHURST 1858-1928

Little did you foresee when as a suffragette,
you fought the struggle for women's liberty.
The subservient woman hath now evolved,
the gentle submissive female now extinct,
Her inhibitions no longer asleep or oppressed,

they have been released,
congruous to a volcanic eruption,
gushing forth with profound energy
and amazing splendour.

She strives to succeed in a world once dominated by men,
It was just a dream of your era then.
Whilst on her journey to sovereignty,
she must make time to procreate,
before her biological clock whispers,
it is too late.

A mate or partner be of no consequence or dilemma,
expressive love to be consummated,
no longer the final option.
Baby's conception can be induced,
by artificial insemination.

Then her sweet child of innocence,
will have several mentors to hold the umbilical reigns.
Alas, family life may never be the same again.

Yes Emily we have progressed,
the female takes little rest.
She is the hunter of her pride,
self sufficiency her prey,
her femininity no longer as fragile as glass,
compared to womankind of the past.

E Dobie

Here To Stay

Votes for women
Came the cry,
Horror, disbelief, unheard of,
Run, hide,
Recognised demonstrating,
Impossible,
Woman's place, home.

Furrows of war,
Presence felt, tilling soil,
Cultivating land,
Posted front line, administer
To wounded.
Secret service, incognito,
Sheltering homeless.

Families part, children distraught,
Mum's around she will sort out,
Call for mum, or women alike
Is endless,
Be inclined, please, let them speak.

Roll of a woman, covers many spheres,
Changes occur, status emerges,
Equality, for what, or whom,
Self impose, build, unite,
Establish firm foundations,
Silver lining, mainstay, hope,
A reliable anchorage.

Lorna Tippett

'Masters' Degree In Women's Studies

I hope some day my dissertation
Has some effect upon the nation
And not be hid - for few to see
Inside some dusty library!

For four years now my banner's furled
On injustice in 'a woman's world'.
From early primary socialisation
And discrepancies in education,
And, how to fit in culturally
She seeks a job - but *primarily*
Her really greatest expectation
Is to increase the population
And be dependant on a man
Then work *part*-time just when she can . . .

The potential boss, at interview
Will very simply take his cue
On pure and simple gender traits
To govern just how much he pays -
For: 'What she earns is additional
To the family wage from her husband's skill
And will be spent on luxuries . . .
Whilst *his* is for necessities'!

Her working wage and occupation
Are ruled by g-e-nderi-sa-tion.
If she's under-educated and has no skill
It's presumed the 'mother-role' she'll fill.

And so (unless she's born elite)
It really means she can't compete
Against men's skill and higher wages
(They've had it good since Feudal ages!)

So - a woman's life perspective's damned
By man's iron sword in his velvet hand . . .
(To look towards some restitution
Read: Beechey's ('82) solution).

Hannah Yates

A Woman's World?

When we were young, - *Dad* was head of the house
We did not dispute it - it was the *norm,*
For any decisions or queries, - it was always, - *'Ask your Dad'*
It was that way, - from the day we were born.

In today's world, - the wheel has turned, a full circle
Now, - it's *Mum* - who rules the house,
Dad - has become a *yes* and *no* man
For conversation, - he is as quiet as a mouse.

Once, long ago, - *men* were dominant, - but today
Equality, - has changed all that,
Where *men* once called a meeting, - a *conference*
Today, - *women,* - go along for a chat.

In the *commons,* - there is a female *speaker*
There are *lady magistrates, - traffic wardens,* and *police,*
And in high summer, - you will find a *lady* clad in white
Batting, - at the crease.

Now, - as we near the 21st century, - women have taken the initiative
Man, - has taken a back seat,
It is happening in *politics,* - in *sport,* - and *religion*
It is happening, - in every street.

In the *home, - factory,* - or *office*
It is *she,* - who *must* be obeyed,
But remember, it is a *woman's* privilege to change her mind
When the *final plans,* - have all been made.

Bertha Gold

WOMEN TODAY

Women from time immemorial
Have been the strongest voice
Nations have been governed
By the will of a woman's choice
In the reign of Cleopatra
Many a man did cower
She was a politician true
Who manipulated her power
But many times it has been
The woman with the softest voice
Who's made a man move mountains
To cancel the deeds of vice
And now two thousand years after
Women have changed their place
Politics, medicine and business,
Are improved by a woman's grace
No longer type-cast in the roll of a mother
Confined to that ancient fate
They've progressed to another standing
Is this their ultimate fate?
Equality, fraternity seems to sum it up
And of course the gentle touch
Has been long since recognised
Because women give so much!

Moira M Michie

OAP

I'm sometimes called an OAP
But a senior citizen is also me
I'll never forget those far off days
It's good to remember the quiet ways
But now it's my feet they worry me so
The bleak winter months I always did dread
When cold winds kept blowing all round my head
It must be because my blood's getting thin
I'm putting on two of everything
The boys and the girls they all seem so bold
It must be a sign that I'm getting old
Now it's out in the open, the things kept hid
Each story is told to the highest bid
My feet are still hurting I'll sit down a while
To think of the things that caused me to smile
I'll always be thankful for the things that I had
And I never would change my mum or my dad
The pound always bought you really good fare
But the shops that you knew would always be there
When my legs start to ache I can get on a bus
Then show them my pass and it's free without fuss
I wish that the traffic would slow down a mite
When I want to cross over it gives me a fright
Why do they build the buildings so tall
I'll always be thinking they are all going to fall
We are happy to move at a slower pace
And really don't want to be first in the race
The young and the old must find peace as they live
For each single one has a blessing to give

May Walker

Daughters Of Selene

Selene, fair goddess of the silver moon
Touched barren earth's bleak, cold skin,
A brought forth from the darkened void
A girl child in her likened form
Divine, and yet in earthly shape,
First fruit upon the arid earth,
First Eve of all womankind.
And yet this fragrant dream of fair Selene,
Whose godly thought bore temporal flesh
To live beneath her silvery glance,
Yearned so for a brother soul,
And wakened from the slumbers of the night
The sun's bright god to reach and fashion from the dust
An earthly mate to live and mingle with her heart,
Her moisture to his air, her coolness to his heat,
Her loveliness to sate his mortal longing
And create within his mind and soul,
The seed of human life, conceived in flesh,
And carried, nurtured in such sacred vessel
That is woman, daughter of night's goddess moon.

Beverley Ann Fairfoull

UNTITLED

When I am older much older
Than now
I'll play Elvis Presley as
Loud as I can.
I'll have lots of parties just
For the homeless, wear big round
Badges saying *people come first,*

My favourite reading will be
Comics galore to be read only
In church on a Sunday.

I'll dye my hair purple, orange or green,
Then walk through the town singing
        'Only Sixteen'.
I'll spend a whole day in Marks and Spencer
Riding up and down on the escalator.

I'll use any excuse to go off on a march,
Waving a banner saying *'I don't give a toss.'*

I'll go out in rain storms splashing in puddles
Eat two bubble gum at once blowing big bubbles,
And every house that I pass I'll ring
Their doorbell then run up the street
Like a bat out of hell.

I'll stand in the police station shouting
        'My dog is missing!'
And hours later say 'I was only kidding.'

I'll lose my money most every day
And tell my children 'It's your turn to pay.'
        But for now I must
        Wait patiently
        Oh I really can't wait
        To reach seventy!

Vi White

THOUGHTS AT TRECASTELL

Thinking thoughts in my summer head,
No need to worry with thoughts of dread,
Of things to do and say and be,
Just feel the breeze, the country, the sea.
This is me now inside my head, no clock to watch
And dates to meet, obliged to stay in a one-way street.
I can drift and daydream as I please,
Me alone with the summer trees.
I like my town life well enough
It's busy, hectic, not dream-like stuff.
When I am there, I feel it's me,
Or what's expected for all to see.
But in my mind, perhaps other's too,
I feel there's more to see and do.

Jean Phillips

I'M NOT BITTER

Why *should* I be bitter?
I've had a better chance than most.
I ran alongside the best of them -
Just missed the winning post.

Why *should* I be bitter?
It was never *my* fault.
My *body* wasn't up to it,
So I *had* to call a halt.

Who *said* that I was bitter?
It's just that I turn cold,
Watching cars (as they drive past)
Dodge a *streetwise* three year old!

Who said that *they* were better?
And let *them* have a child.
I *know* I'd make a better mum,
It just makes me feel *wild!*

Oh no, no, I'm *not* bitter.
But I wish *they'd* understand,
What a *blessing* their children are
And give them a guiding hand!

Meanwhile, a family knitter,
Made a shawl for my big *non-event,*
It will keep me warm when I'm old and grey.
(Although that wasn't her intent.)

I really try not to be bitter.
But sometimes I'm under a cloud.
And sometimes I long for what I can't have.
So, a moan, now and then is allowed.

Penny Treble

THIS IS YOUR LIFE

'This is your life' live it now!
Don't waste time wondering how
How you'll manage, what you'll be
Trust in God implicitly.

Make the most of every hour
Watch each precious moment flower,
Smell the scent that comes with living
Laughing, crying, sharing, giving.

Don't waste time wondering 'why'
This made you laugh, that made you cry,
Don't say 'If only I'
If is a word that will make you cry.

Take this gift, this gift of life
Share with lover, husband, wife,
Mother, father, child or friend,
Share it wisely it will end.

Reincarnation may come to pass
You may return but then alas!
You won't return as you are now
This is your life, live it now.

Aggie McGinty

THE AGE OF EQUALITY

Being a woman in today's world
Is a very tough role indeed.
Whether a working mum or housewife
Our workload would make a man reel.
Now this is the age of equality
Well that's what we're lead to believe
But, every sensible woman
Knows this is not how we feel
So what does the male
Really want from us
Read on you may get a buzz
A hostess for their business dinners
A nurse to fuss them when they're ill
A maid to clean fetch and carry
A cook who keeps them full and happy
A woman for all seasons
One who listens to reason
Lets them watch the sport on telly
Go out with their mates for a bevy
Arrive home in a state
Get up very late
Keep what they earn a state secret
Let us use the car when they don't need it
We get up when the baby cries
They turn over onto their sides
We go to school and meet the kids' teacher
Taking care of their futures
Doing this makes us look quite old
But not them the lucky souls
They get themselves a newer model
With low mileage and lots of bottle
They want to be dominated you see
Is this what is meant by equality.

Ann Hunter

UNTITLED

Something I have always failed to see,
why she always knew what was best for me.
I had dreams and aspirations of what I'd be and what I'd do
she knew better though, the more I dreamed the less I grew.
I was steered and was manoeuvred, she moulded me a style
reality saw dreams and fantasies in a shattered pile.

Trust and love gave way to insecurities and fears,
trust and love that turned to anger with the passing of the years.

Please let me be where I know I must be,
don't waste precious time trying to live your life through me.
The cord must be severed before I turn blue,
we are two different persons, I am I you are you.

Karen Molyneux

WOMEN'S OPINIONS

Young, old, middle-aged too,
Remember you all have a right to a view.
So stand up, and speak out on what you feel right
It's time that you all started joining the fight.

The young Miss today studies hard to progress,
But she still follows fashion, likes to be smart of dress.
She dreams of a future that's happy, secure,
But must proudly declare, it's to last evermore.

The mums and the middle-aged all would agree,
That life can be hectic hard working are they.
They all want their rights, and a happiness shared.
If they all shout out loudly then they will be heard.

So come on you women and strongly unite,
It's time to speak up and show off your might
All get together regardless of age;
And give your opinions a really full page.

R Anderson

Child Of My Dream

You're the child of my dream I await your birth.
My body it swells you're growing there.
I hope, how I pray that you will come to birth.
The months they go swiftly till at four months there's pain.
I go to the doctor's perhaps he'll explain.
But the doctor examines me 'Your child lies there dead.
I'll send you to hospital a miscarriage.' he said.
I laid on a stretcher shaking with such dread.
Thinking of my other children a lying on their beds.
How can I say to them all your brother is dead.
The doctors walk in say what's all the grief.
You've four kids at home one less to feed.
So off they all go leaving me alone to grieve.
Then my specialist arrives with reading machine.
The nurse rubs jelly on my belly all around.
What he has there is early ultra-sound.
He bows his head I think he's saying a prayer.
Suddenly we both hear your heart beat there.
In my womb thirty weeks you then did stay.
Till I went into labour one night in May.
They told me then your heart had stopped.
But in giving you birth it started again with shock.
A tiny boy you turned out to be.
Now you're a strong man of six foot three.

B Bonner

A Mother's Task

What is he doing, where is he now?
Am I wrong to even ask?
What I should know, now he's a man
is how well I've completed my task.

I cared for him and nursed him,
Taught him all I knew.
From babyhood to manhood
I guided as he grew.

Teenage years weren't easy,
he was hard to understand.
Was guidance right, is he thankful,
or did I fail in my command?

I prayed for help and guidance,
and did the best I could.
Now he's a man I still advise,
while wondering if I should.

When is a mother's task over?
Am I but a spectator now?
Do I take a back seat graciously,
or leave the stage with a bow?

To the world he's a man, to me my child.
For him I still love and care.
I pray my son lives a happy life,
If he needs me, I'll be there.

Marie Nelson

It's A Medical Fact

Women don't need to be treated with tact!
Don't take my word; it's a medical fact.
Women don't cry but hormonal tears
Caused by oversupply of oil to their gears.
Women can't feel pain - the way that men do!
It's a short circuit that makes them faint in the loo.
Women are androids, and androids often dysfunction.
Women would know this if they had any gumption.
Women are nought percent human; it's a medical fact,
Published worldwide, sometimes in hardback.
But I didn't find out from books written for men:
Shh! When doctors weren't listening, I heard it from them.

Sharon Marie Johnston

TRAPPED

Time seems to be suspended
  he doesn't hear my voice
My body is locked in irons
  unable to express
The fear that I am trapped
  and cannot find the key

My needs, my cares, my life
  do not appear to matter
Whatever questions I utter
  fall like lead
In still dark limpid waters
  buried in the silt

Can't he sense the ripples
  surely they are felt
Skimming along like a stone
  or do they disappear
Swallowed by dark despair

Perhaps I should make waves
  muddy up the shore
Make sure they surge higher
  thunderous and raw
I have to break the bondage
  break free for once and all

Margaret Sturgess

Woman's Lot

Sometimes a woman's lot
is not a happy one
if she marries too soon
and loses all the fun
she had in her teens
while walking out
with the man of her dreams

But make no mistake
let me get one thing clear
she'll marry this man
if it takes her all year
to persuade him.

Adelaide June Marshall

LADY WINTER

Welcome Lady Winter
in your long dark dress
your bare white feet
and silver face,

striding through the iron
furrows of the field,
cold stars crackling
from your hair.

Martha Street

IRRITATED

How does my hair look?
Does this make me look fat?
You're not wearing them,
Can't be seen dead in that.

Don't I look lovely?
My hair-dye, my make-up,
You're looking so plain,
Still, they won't notice you.

Look what she's wearing,
Armani, Calvin Klein,
Very reasonable,
Almost as good as mine.

You look so frumpy,
Can't you buy some new clothes?
Only essentials,
Can't you borrow some more?

The scream and the hairspray linger in the air.
The noise of the bullet made people stare.
Blood adds its colour to bottle blonde hair.
Gets twenty years but she just doesn't care.
No fashion tips in the cell she must share.

Ann-Marie Johnson

THE CHANGE

The biggest secret of them all
Till it suddenly hits you like a thunderbolt
The menopause they whisper low
I'm not really old enough, so I don't really know,
They kid themselves and pretend
But it's going to get them in the end
If they told the truth, and helped each other
To know we're not alone, with all this bother
From bags of energy raring to go
Now I'm permanently, on a go slow
I go to the doctor's, they don't want to know
I'm flushing and sweating, and feeling so low
I wish I lived where there's plenty of snow
Wear cotton clothes so I change my attire
But here I am still feeling on fire
I can give you something to help with the sweats
But they can cause dizziness as side affects
With that in mind I declined
I was thinking of trying HRT
Oh you don't really need it just eat healthily
I'm trying now to lose some weight
As all my joints are starting to ache
My friend's just gone on HRT
The one that's made from pregnant mares' wee
She's *galloping* round and feeling great
Saying why don't you try it for goodness sake
Is it safe, will it set me free
Or cure me of everything and just kill me

D McGeer

ANOREXIC

There she stands,
Vision of the 20th century ideal,
The figure most women
Would die for.

Starved into oblivion,
A walking corpse,
Eyes sunken into deep, dark caverns,
Jutting cheek bones and
Paper-like skin
Stretched tight across the wreck of her face.

Body protruding sharply,
Angular, brutal,
Shoulders drooping, forwards,
As if to hide the ruins beneath.
Concave chest and brittle legs
Barely holding her up.
Head bowed to hide the shame
Of her 'fatness'.

This is how a woman should be
Cry the voices in the night
'Slim and beautiful'
'Beautiful and slim.'
Anything but
Fat!

Desperation clenches her tired heart,
Haunted eyes stare inwards
Into the storms within her mind.
A wasted shadow of her former self.
Emaciated, lonely, aching.

Smiling memories flit by like petals on the breeze,
Hunger screams in the chasm of
Emptiness.

A fading flower,
Her light dimming,
Success is hers in the eyes of the world
The only acceptance from the living
Is to sacrifice herself by dying.

Anon

A Woman's Touch

His wife had died, he
had explained but
her presence can
still be felt
in the moonlit room.

A silver framed wedding
portrait and feminine
things adorn the bedroom;
a powder bowl, half full
and a satin gown.

A perfume of flowers
and musk sweetly
scent the air, whilst
her lover sleeps
exhausted from their passion.

A tiny bunch of
fragrant violets
add a woman's touch,
remembrance of the wife
he had loved, so much.

She slips from the bed
and silently dresses.
The bride in the
silver frame watches
as she leaves the room.

Jane Leeming

Votes For Women

How often have we heard them say
I never vote, never, why should I?
I know nothing of politics in any way
I let elections pass me by.

Do they not know of women brave
Who suffered - yes and even died
To get the vote that women craved
To make us equal in all eyes?

So ladies use your vote and fight
To keep the faith with those brave souls
Who fought so hard for women's rights
And we can more easily reach our goals.

The aim is peace for women everywhere
To keep their menfolk safe from war,
So make your voices heard, show you care
That in future, wars will be no more.

Emma Hunt

EQUALITY

What is equality?
We all get exactly the same.
Would we want that?
If it really came.
Can we really expect it?
If it goes by that name.
It's the dream of everyone young.
Yet the word itself should be hung.
Why dream of an impossible concept?
When it goes beyond what we can expect.

J Haywood

Ode To The Unborn

Sorry my sweet one I bid you goodnight
Your birthright was taken and you couldn't fight
But please do forgive me for what I have done
It hurts me so deeply my daughter or son

Your life was created unplanned and unknown
I wish I could have stopped before your seed was sown
If souls go a-floating I hope you will rest
In knowing I did what I thought was the best

Not a day will go by when you are not in my head
And I think of the words that I could have said
The fear of wondering if I was right
Will haunt me forever through day and by night

But now you are taken protected from pain
And I pray that your life was not taken in vain
My heart will be aching 'til the day that I die
But for my other children I really must try
So when you see me living and laughing again
Be sure under the surface I will still feel the pain

Debbie Connor

A Woman

W from the womb
O from the ovary
M for a male
A from ancestor
N for never ending.

A Bhambra

A Man Is Only A Man

Women now are more free
Than we used to be
But men are the same
So how can you gain?

This is not a comment
On women who famously paint and write
Women in high places,
Achievements, since the vote.

But your average Ms.
Who's always under stress,
Working and wifing
And mothering maybe
Doing all jobs with house and baby.
There's another free woman just looking for a man
If the fun's run out
Of his present plan.

Jo Appleyard

THE OTHER WOMAN . . .
(Dedicated to Niki Moone)

There she sits despondently
Wondering if he'll show
But unexpectedly there was snow
So perhaps she'll never know . . .

She ponders silently. Recalling his features
Oh that heart breaking smile
But would he go
The extra mile . . .

Her pint watered down with soda
It had broken down . . . her Skoda . . .
Just had to make her drink last
Can't afford to be out drinking all night
What with the kids in bed and that . . .
But would he just smell a rat . . .

He'd written her number
On a beer mat
Now she's sat wondering
Where he's at . . .

Or if he even remembers her
Or just one glamorous wave of passion
He burst through the door . . . smoothing down his hair
Gulped rapidly for air
He moves towards her . . . arms outstretched . . .

. . . Late . . . office . . . smiles . . . wife . . . a lame excuse
She stubs out her cigarette
And looks keenly into his eyes
Oh how blatantly he lies
But what can she say . . . she knew she was . . . the other . . . woman

Sally Wyatt

THE HIGH COLUMN BROKEN

'Rotto e l'alta colonna e il verde lauro'

Over many years
These words have haunted me.
I have lived with the high column broken
And the green laurel
Fallen. I have lived with the ruins.

Carefully, slowly, sadly
I have built a life -
First beside them
Then later, over them.

Now there is this life,
Smooth, like a green mound
Grassed over with the
Accumulation of years
Of living: jobs and children and work and play.

Who will ever uncover
Under the plump hillocks and grassy slopes
The pain of the high column broken
And the green laurel
Fallen?

Maureen Cawdron

Russian Cup With Scarlet Tulips

The cup restored,
appears more fragile now,
its hurt reduced to tiny hairline scars.
So beautiful!
It paid the consequence
for such seduction
but knit together well
beneath your hands.

On opposite sides
two vivid, scarlet tulips
reach out to touch
across the curve of
molten black.

What palette gave you form?
What inward eye?
We need no gift of tongues
to share the dance,
Let pour the nectar
and never mind the cracks.

Daphne Kirkpatrick

The Ogre

An ogre lives here.
I cook his meals, and after
Dinner, he snoozes.

He is gentle, yet
Like living under a volcano,
I shudder in awe and expectation.

He walks quietly, but
His vibration I sense
Everywhere.

My squeaks annoy him.
And when he is away
I grow in stature.

The more he is away
The more I grow.
When he returns, I shrink.

How can I get him to
Stay away a long long time?
Then I, too, can become an ogre.

Angela Brennan

A Perfect Match

I was told many years ago,
A woman's work was to cook and sew,
Clean the house, look after your man,
Always do the best that you can.

This I did, but to no avail,
This merely led to a marriage fail.
Three times more I did endeavour,
Then I vowed, never, never.

Then this man with eyes of brown,
On one knee did he go down,
He said to me 'Forget the rest,'
Because, with him I had the best.

As years went by I did discover,
There was more than being a wife and mother,
All the tasks he did share,
I became free as air.

Instead of two, one are we,
Living life as it should be,
Rock solid is he and my best friend,
On my partner, I can depend.

Jacqueline Coman

We've Got It Made

In days gone by, a woman's role
Was to serve her man and get the coal
She'd be a slave and a baby machine
Cook all meals and keep house clean

If they could return for a nosey
They'd agree the 90s are quite cosy
The washboard is now history
With thanks to electricity

We don't have to poke the fires
We're modern now and all live wires
There's no need to beat the rugs
We just switch on at the plugs

There's central heating and fridge freezers
Plenty hot water (clever geysers)
Vacuum cleaners, tumble dryers,
Most anything our heart desires

These appliances are all time saving
They'd be amazed at microwaving
And think our life is full of thrills
(Well so it is - till we get the bills!)

Everything is easier now
Stand up you ladies and take a bow
We just don't know how you coped
For a better life, you must have hoped

You'd be surprised at life today
It's much better in every way
Good birth control too, yes siree!
There's the pill or a vasectomy

We keep our men on the hop
'Do what you're told or get the chop.'
C'mon now boys, don't be sour
What we have now is Girl Power!

Ruth Le-Vallois

UNITE

You look at me and what do you see?
Black, white, Asian or English,
I am united with everyone of you
because I am a woman!
I know how it feels to love and hate,
to be rejected or wanted,
because I am a woman!
I can sympathise with you
when you are hurt,
and have been used,
because I am a woman!
I can put myself in your shoes
and I know what to say to
ease the pain,
because I am a woman!
I know why you like shopping,
talking on the phone for hours,
and eating tubs of ice-cream
when you are upset,
because I am a woman!
We have that special bond
that unites us all,
no matter what race.
We can be there for each other
because we are women!

Khatija Navsa

TERRA INCOGNITA

I am a woman
who gropes about
into space beyond
the bars of a vow
I am a woman
who stops looking
in front and after
my loved ones
I am a woman
who starts braining
and changing
awareness
I am a woman
who was owned
and now is
my future
I am a woman
who will not fear
will not waver
will not retreat
I am a woman
who will not pay
any price for
being loved
I am a woman
who offers this life
for glowing with
'nsatiable curiosity
I am a woman
taking possession
slow motion
of terra incognita

Candal Danzabel

Jenny Is Homeless

I'm glad I'm a Nobody
For Nobody cares
If I sit on the pavement
With lice in my hair.

I once had a home
With a Mum and Dad,
But Dad went to Heaven
And that made us sad,

Now Mum's got a boyfriend
Much younger than she,
And when Mum's not looking
He tries to molest me.

I'm cold and I'm hungry
And long for the bed
I slept in so safely
Before Dad was dead.

So when you pass by
With your nose in the air,
Be glad you're a Someone
With clean shining hair.

Margaret Carl Hibbs

Double Standards

It doesn't matter you're a girl
Until things go wrong
Then the guys start singing
A very different song.

She's a tart
But he's a lad
The way people think
Is really sad.

She's at fault
Cos she's got the baby
He'll never get blamed
Not even maybe.

They'll say if you
Get anywhere
You did it
By the 'director's' chair.

But though it may
Take an eternity
One day we'll
Know equality.

Kim Prince Wilkerson

UNTITLED

Blue striped school boys
standing in rows,
mud splattered trainers
with holes in the soles,
bags flung carelessly
over their shoulders,
over-spilling with
crisp bags and folders,
shirt tails hanging and
wind flapping ties,
laughing, dirty faces
and excitement in eyes,
where will they be in
nine or ten years?
Life on the line
their heads in their beers,
hand to mouth with
downcast head,
a wife in the kitchen
the children in bed.

Amanda J George

EXPECTATIONS

My husband expects me to be there for him
To do the cooking, the washing, the cleaning
And of course my love light must never dim
And not forgetting to stay nice and slim.

My children expect devotion unending
So for the next twenty years my life I'll be spending
To all of their various needs I'll be tending
Am I a good mother, the verdict's still pending.

My parents expect a doting daughter
They're old now and need looking after
All these extra duties incline to make my day shorter
Sometimes I feel like a lamb to the slaughter.

My friends all expect a listening ear
Brimming with advice and loads of good cheer
My friends are all nice and I hold them all dear
But sometimes I wish my problems they'd hear.

At work they expect an uprising star
Who puts everything in to promoting her career
So for five days a week I push myself far
But to me it's a treadmill that pays for the car.

The whole world expects me to answer their need
I'm only one person, but they don't see
I spend my whole life running from A back to B
And nobody realises the demands placed on me.

S K Clark

Don't Muzzle The Mouths Of Your Women

Don't muzzle the mouths of your women.
The Spirit rests where He will.
The woman gathered with the disciples at Pentecost,
For the Holy Spirit their beings to fill.

We read of Huldah, the prophetess,
In the Old Testament of God's word.
The priest and men of high rank
Had to be instructed by her from the Lord.

It seems the first preacher of Jesus was a woman.
The prophetess Anna spread the news of His birth,
'To all them that looked for redemption in Jerusalem,'
Free redemption for all of the earth.

Mary Magdelene was the first person to see Jesus,
After He arose from the dead.
He had saved her from sin, made her pure within.
She was the first preacher of His resurrection, 'tis said.

'Ye are all one in Christ Jesus'. The Bible tells us so.
Man, woman, or child who receive Him are given the
commission to 'Go'
'Into all the world, to preach the gospel to every creature'.
Any of them can become a teacher, or a preacher.

It is a sin to silence the woman.
The Spirit rests where He will,
How can they obey the Holy Spirit
If they're told to sit silent and still.

Some churches who ban women speaking
Send lady missionaries alone, far to roam,
In great dangers, to preach to the natives.
What hypocrisy, when they're kept silent at home.

W R Pettitt

Stolen Moments

I was afraid to bite into forbidden pleasure,
you, the sweet fruit on my plate.
I savour your taste at my leisure,
placed there by a twist of fate.

The awakening that stirs within my heart,
like your smile that caresses me all over.
The yearning pain when we're apart,
then entering becomes a Super Nova.

A glimpse chases the emptiness from my life,
and your honey sweetness an opiate to my senses.
Dreams cradle me throughout the night,
but in daylight there are no pretences

Stolen moments within your arms are heaven,
with secret kisses upon my lips and face.
Arousing our bodies with a passionate longing,
our hunger only melts when we are sate.

Joan Lister

Eternal Dove

Christ - the Holy King of women
who teach all in your name
who tend their worlds to honour
Your glory and eternal fame.
Christ - the Holy King of women
look down and bless them true
in mercy be their strength
as they call and seek only you
be their feet at stumbling times
and their joy at praise,
always hold them dearly
as they defend the born of these days
Lord, be their flaming arrow
to strike the foe at night,
lest the day brings trouble
Holy Spirit guide their sight.
Forgiveness is Your humbling stream
smile on them, Lord of Grace
let them loving you, beam
telling women of Your Kingship and love
comforting ways of faith
that come from You their Eternal Dove.

Linda Daly

VISION

What do you see when you look at me
my gender, colour and frame
but that isn't really the real me,
it's just the package God chose to wrap me in.
So why not do something really different . . .
take time and the package very gently unwrap.
It may take a while to remove all the casing
for it protects something very fragile inside.
But I'm sure when all the casing is off
a very precious gift you shall find . . .
Then take a step back and look once again,
this time with your heart not your eyes
and then answer this question for me.
What stimulates your interest now?
When you look beyond what you physically see,
is it the package that God wrapped in me
or is it its contents - the real me

Gez Larkin

CRIES IN THE DARK

I am crying in the dark.
For lost loves and lost babies.
For words unsaid, no comfort given.
For broken promises, anger, jealousy.
Feelings unshown, forgiveness withheld.

The dark is sterile emptiness.
I pour out my tears.
But it is water in the sand -
Never full, always seeping away.
Yet my crying never ceases,
It is constant inside.

Tears well up from beneath the ocean.
All the waters of bereavement and loss spill over,
Until the shivering body revolts.
The sobs and cries remain.
Tears swallowed up in grief.
The being shakes without tears.

Lost the initial reason for crying,
Gasping in a paroxysm of grief,
Trying to expel the hurt with breath,
Crying for the world in the indifferent darkness,
But finally, crying just for me . . . alone.

Hilary Garrett

NOT JUST A GIRL

Thought of as nothing by the chauvinistic men.
Thinking I'll be the Barbie and they'll be the Ken.
I am more than a body, I am a mind, a voice.
I am more than an object and I demand a choice.
Why should I wash your clothes and cook you a meal?
Why should women get the unfair deal?
I don't press flowers and I hate the colour pink
Just because I'm a girl, I have to stand by the sink?
I'm not supposed to fight or play footie on the pitch.
Just because I stand up for myself I get brandished a bitch?
If men are so clever, why don't they cook their own food?
Is it beneath them or can they only be rude?
Look at my face when I'm talking to you.
Not my chest.
My eyes tell everything, my body says less.
I am proud of who I am, not just a girl.
But me.

Gemma Bodsworth (16)

GETTING IN PERSPECTIVE

Is it truly, really effective
  Getting things in perspective
Like organising one's only life
Especially if you're a mother and a wife
Organising the children and home
If one intends to roam
To taking up a career
Making money or making ends meet
The family do have to eat
But the woman who is alone
Working her fingers to the bone
Kids to feed, a house to keep
  Keeping them warm with a place to sleep
Has to know her limits
Doesn't have many minutes
To herself, suffer does her health
So she had to really try
To get her life all cut and dry
By getting things in perspective
Certainly is effective
The only way to cope
Or she doesn't have a hope.

T Hartley

Women's Rights

Women have always had to fight
For all that should be theirs by right,
Men are dominant partners you see,
So what's all this talk of equality.

If you pass your test and drive a car,
Men think they are better by far,
Even though statistics can be seen
They'll pass it off and make a scene.

In parliament there are far more men,
We need a balance, let's have more women,
For women have a great deal to offer
And do not need men as a scoffer.

Women are needed in all walks of life
To be a good mother and a wife,
But women are capable beings too
And are well prepared to see things through.

Women should come out to the fore,
And show the world they can do more,
By speaking out with heart and voice
And make sure they're heard by their noise.

If we sit like little Jack Horner
Out of sight and in a corner,
We will never be heard as we should
But end up like a block of wood.

So let the spirit of women shine
Into this world of yours and mine,
We have every right to have our say
And some day we will, come what may.

Vera G Taylor

The Child Within

Snug in my watery home, secure in mother's womb
Hearts beating harmoniously, in union and love.
Muffled sounds I noticed, gentle voices, loving care
Relaxedness, contentment permeate
Via a cord. Totally enveloping.
My security then shattered
As mother's heartbeat changed.
Silenced were the voices, stilled the laughter.
Now body racked with sobs,
Sensitive to mounting tension,
I felt my mother's growing grief
The enormity of her decision
Soon apparent did become.
All natural movement ceased
The walls around mutate, threatening my existence
My fight of life began.
Life which once was so precious, now disagreeable to her
What had wrought about this change?
I comprehended not. I wanted to cry out, 'Stop it!
Mum it's me your daughter' Helpless, silent I remain
To my life I cling, I fight, withholding capitation
Not yielding to her will, my tenacious life within her
Drowsy does become, weak I now have left her,
Suffered both have we.
Burst open then her body, by the surgeon's knife,
A rush of air, the shock of light
My life ends - before begun.

Teresa Booth

Moving Day

Dust and cobwebs is all I found,
As I had a last look round,
Undraped windows, bare cold wall,
Nothing left of mine, at all,
But memories, sweet and sad,
Of happy, good times, and bad.
How much of me is here enshrined,
Hopes and failures, intertwined.
Best close the door, look to the new,
Another home, another view.
Life's full of promise, I'll take heart,
Face the future, make a fresh start.

Daphne White

A First Experience

One Sunday when a little girl
With hair in tight and light brown curl,
My father said 'Our little lass
At three, can come with me to Mass.'

The morning walk was cool and fine,
Just right for peace and thoughts devine.
All entered through the open door
And blessed themselves, both rich and poor,

My father said 'This is God's house,
You must be quiet, just like a mouse,
And kneel upon this wooden place
To say your prayers and ask God's grace.'

I knew the prayer we said at night,
For God to help us do aright,
And Jesus and the Holy Spirit
The Godhead who made just one digit.

But then my childish mind did wander,
And on different footwear ponder,
Those boots and shoes of varied styles
Some new some old, they'd walked for miles.

But murmured prayers were hushed and stilled
With lovely sound the church was filled
With reverberating bells which said
'Our Jesus comes, now bow your head.'

My father bowed my head, I knew
The bell had said what's really true
And so I've kept the faith always
And hope to, till I end my days.

Georgina Ivison

WEDLOCK . . . 1930 . . .

He was the boss, he told her so.
'I earn the brass and you must toe
The line. Your job's to care for me.
I'm the worker, so you see
I hold the purse-strings.'

She was his slave, he let her know
Without some cash, she couldn't go
She cooked and cleaned for many a hour
As he said, he held the power
With the tight purse-strings.

He lost his job, a dreadful shock,
She held the key to turn the lock
And fled from fear to pastures new
Left alone, what could he do
She'd cut the purse-strings.

Muriel Berry

BROODINESS

Maternity beckons -
Great old mother hen
clucks and scratches round
the life and days of those without.

The feeling of wonder -
unique creation, the incredulous act
of which my stomach is capable.

I stroke its roundness from
retention and impending proof
of lack of motherhood.
Imagining life within.
Creating ways of getting my fix.
I crave, but it hurts, it idealises.
Dreams so important are
pushed aside - made never really wanted.
The love, possession, sharing,
growing, overwhelm me.
The pain, the intrusion, the changes,
the realities evade me.
Unreal in the world of
those collecting twigs for the nest.

But spring has gone, or not yet come.
Mating season is out of season.
The mind sinks back into itself,
dealing with the DTs from womb opium.
Logistics evade, realisation confronts,
I wonder of infertility and
the sadness seeps through me.
From toe to head and back to the stomach.
And heart.
Where it is told to stay, imprisoned -
and accepted as what I really want.

But she scratches and struts
round the walls of my womb -
pecking and stabbing
every once in a while . . .
Twisting her head up and sideways
to meet my heart with her eye.

Alison Hawtin-Dumbravá

A QUESTION AN ANSWER

Will the millennium create a new future for me,
No more poverty, destruction, insecurity.

Will the masses learn to live as one,
Discarding their arms dismantling the bomb,

Will the leaders of state learn not to dictate,
To the poor and the needy, scorning their fate,

Will someone listen to the working man's voice,
Helping him realise he does have a choice,

Will the world self destruct at the hands of the few,
Or can we unite and pull ourselves through,

Will the famines in other countries keep going strong,
Or do the food mountains need transporting to where they belong,

Will judgement be made for the sake of us all,
Or is it going to be the rich that don't fall,

Will people still hate the different colours of skin,
Dose it really matter what's on the outside look deep within,

Will man make an oath to cure not kill,
As our air is polluted by the overspill,

Will the dawn and sunset remind me it's day,
As global warming decides the weather today,

Will my family be safe in the next century,
A question an answer which will it be.

Debbie Cauch

IF SHE GAVE YOU HER HEART!

If she gave you her heart,
Would you feel her beating softly?
Would your heart beat softly with hers?
Two to beat as one,
A pulsating sun.

If she gave you her mind,
Would your mind climb in and take over her dreams?
Would she become part of your dreams too?
To become part of you.

If she gave you her body,
Would you hold her and feel her need and her passion?
Would your body need and receive what she has to give?
To fulfil her need, to help her live.

If she gave you her soul,
Would you keep it safe and uphold her spirit?
Would you give her your spirit and soul?
To be together, to become whole.

If she gave you her life,
Would you nurture her, take care of her and help her to grow?
Would you wish to be with her and see how your life would be?
What would happen if I gave you me?

Helen Mckenna

THE CHANGE

The changing moods of womanhood
Are something quite apart,
We have our highs, we have our lows
And palpitating hearts,
The changing emotions
Are sometimes hard to bear,
It might be a little easier
If your problems you can share,
There are times you feel so down
That no-one can understand,
That every irritability
Needs a helping hand,
You can feel suicidal
Just pouring out the tears
If only we could realise
Other women have these fears,
We know we can come through it
But at times it's just sheer hell,
How long it lasts, how deep the mood
No-one can really tell,
For some the change is easier
Without the doubt and fear,
But for those who have a struggle
They need to know help's near,
They need to know there's others
That feel they way they do,
And that there's women everywhere
Know what they're going through.

Lilian Summers

A Woman's World

Is it here now? No just for some,
A woman's world is yet to come.
A world where we are equal as men,
A world for all women. not the one in ten.

Women are the child bearers,
Women are the child carers.
We have cared for the young and the old,
The sick and those left out in the cold.

Women have cared in the past,
Women will no doubt care in the future.
Let us be recognised at last,
Let recognition be part of our culture.

The battle is almost won, we're halfway there,
We can't give up now, if we really care.
Fight on, oh army of women fight on,
The battle of the sexes is still to be won.

Patricia Dickson

Boo To The Zoo

I'm wondering what I can do
To those who support the zoo
A breach of animal rights
Imposing unacceptable plights

Captured in their own domain
Transported for human gain
Sad creatures deprived and caged
Humanity should be enraged

Don't tell me they're cared for and fed
Better that most were dead
Look in their sad, sad eyes
Listen to their anguished cries

Many are unable to breed
Fear and misery spread to their seed
Every happening hard to bear
Pounding, no hope, despair

Imprisoned, deprived, confined
Confused in body and mind
Yearning for wild open space
Languid limbs to stretch and race

How would you like the reverse?
Can you think of anything worse?
To be seized and left in the wild
Lost, endangered, defiled

I can't shoot or fight or invade
Bomb the zoo and those who aid
But can proclaim by anger and word
I can shout, I protest, have you heard?

Sheila Beatrice King

WOMEN'S VOICES

Mary Magdalen: 'Sin and hell emptied of its rewards,
the crucified Lord emerged from the shroud
just as gold burned in fire comes out bright as a dozen suns.
The memory of womanhood inscribed in his mind, bodily
from conception to death in love only,
for no woman had scourged, flogged, crucified his tender flesh,
the risen Christ first appeared to me.
His victorious light reverberated on me, stunned in a daze,
yet never more sane.
Hungrily I ate every detail of the beloved face, so familiar and so new.
I wish I could be more true to him and to you,
aware as I am that only the living word can make meaningful my
limited words.'

A woman prays: 'Risen Lord, however dear your hold womanhood,
women have still to struggle for a part to play,
some are still on the threshold.
As unsharing is such a pitfall, liberate us all
so that we can be ready to leap into the new,
share you to bring about a new Resurrection.'

Another woman prays: 'God, men having declared you dead,
with a penny whistle I cannot play well
I have to tell your eternal rhythm.
Yet accept my boldness and penny whistle noise
in memory of your Son and his Mother,
whose unconditional 'Yes' to you, knit your Will to that
of a woman of the deepest heart and the most daring trust
to fit with happiness every age.
To mother the life to come a new song will be sung.
It will bless the earth, lap up the sea and rise.
It will become a universal glorious prayer of praise.'

Angela Cutrale Matheson

SORTING THINGS OUT WITH HIM

Somewhere between what I thought I said
And what he thought he heard
Is what I should have said.

Somewhere between the words I actually said
And those he actually heard
Is what I tried to say.

What I want him to understand never reaches him.
Words never leave me without the softening
Of what I feel I ought to think.

What reaches him does so through his own
Methods of interpretation,
His fixed ideas of me.

So we don't communicate.
Because I am not all he thinks I am,
Because I modify and he interprets:
I don't say and he doesn't listen.

Chris Sanderson

THE NONAGENARIAN

Life still goes on, though different by far
from that which I knew so very long ago;
my values underwent sea-change, some died -
while others lived but hid their battle-scars.

I lived through two world wars; my husband fought
in Egypt, to protect the truths we cherished.
We women learnt to do the work of men,
and, in the learning, other dreams were bought -

and paid for . . . we became more masterful,
more certain of ourselves, and sought to choose
the right to take control and free our lives -
turning our mindless into our meaningful . . .

No battle has had more casualties it seems;
cold gender war became an all-out fight.
And the values of all who had simply stood and waited
passed into history with an Empire's dreams.

But decadence itself decays and sours;
amongst the angst and dross I still perceive
the need for hope and faith, love's old sweet song -
dead dreams reborn, to grow again and flower.

J M Service

ZORA

('The holiness of the heart's affections' John Keats, in a letter to Benjamin Bailey, 22 November 1817)

From woman to woman - of course
that's mainly person to person -
this is a tribute to Zora. Force
of circumstances typical
of this century, which is fierce
on many (how many?) people in the cyclical
upheavals, crises, wars,
murders, wounds and unhealed scars,
all those forces, plus a particular missile,
ruined her home. She did not smile
for many months. Came
by devious routes to work as a cleaner
(she had been a lawyer) - you could say it's a shame.
She probably doesn't believe in a Redeemer.
She relies,
it shows in her eyes,
on something within.

To the lost of the world she is kin.

Judith Hubback

Sea Shore

Clean dry burning pebbles,
Leading down to a sandy shore,
Soft foam-like waves,
Approaching you, teasing your toes then some more.

The smell of ocean seaweed,
Left behind by the ebbing tide,
While little sandcrabs dart away,
Beneath the rocks to hide.

No bottles, cans or glass left here,
The beaches and coast so clean,
But alas, those were the days gone by,
Perhaps like you've never seen.

Now all we have is sewage,
Sometimes floating on the sea,
Tons of trash and rotting food,
Thrown overboard, deliberately.

No seashells can I find now,
No cockles for my tea,
It's a long time now since I came across,
Little winkles from the sea.

We can only hope and pray,
One day things will change,
And let's all hope it won't be long,
Before the sea is clean again.

Amelia Simms

ALL BECAUSE OF YOU!

There you go again, treading on my dreams.
Always the same, or so it seems.
Once upon a time two people were one,
minds thought alike, love just begun.
Now you seem distant, cold all the time.
Treading along on these dreams of mine.
'What's happened to us?' I asked you today.
You just shrugged your shoulders, said you're OK.
What has happened to love, to dreams,
I once thought were true? Now they've all gone.
All because of you!

Zarah Hunter Smith

MATCHES

I read a story, years ago,
About a match girl in the snow,
Selling matches for a penny
And no-one ever buying any.
She lit a match, and by its light
Was treated to a wondrous sight
Of families, and festive cheer,
And people she had held most dear.
The story's end was bitter-sweet,
She died there, on that frosty street.
The angels set her spirit free
And took her from her misery.
Now here I sit, 'neath falling snow,
No family left, nowhere to go.
A scruffy mongrel warms my toes,
And presses to my hand his nose.
Extreme cold makes my body ache;
My hands and feet too cold to shake.
I have no matches in my hands
With which to visit magic lands,
Or see visions of a friendly face
Who'll take me to a better place.
A cardboard box, my only bed.
A pavement pillow for my head.
No warming fire, no Christmas fare,
No presents from the ones who care.
No carols sung around the tree.
Christmas holds no joy for me.
Of future prospects, I have none.
Dreams, ambitions, all are gone.
No reasons left to go on living,
But Christmas is a time for giving,
So if you see me don't walk by.
Give me a match, and let me die.

Jan Lingard

Life's Treasures

Jasmine, whose precious gift perfumes the night,
And honeysuckle too, which lifts its scent upon the dew.
The rose, all glory brings unto the day,
Its fragrance lingers on, and on, upon the way
Through God's magnificent garden of life.
These are my treasures
No money spent,
The beauty of this world is mine,
I am content.

Valerie Clegg

LEFT LUGGAGE

I am looking out of my bedroom window watching the sky,
golden clouds scudding quickly, glinting in the evening
sun for the last few moments. It reminds me of our last
sunset together, and those memories came flooding back.
It is more than a week ago that we stood close together
quietly watching the sun disappear in the western sky,
the end of a day adding poignancy to our imminent parting;
I was to remain behind, as though rooted in the earth,
whilst you seek pastures new and adventure.

How I long to be with you now, as I ponder at the forces
that prevent us from seeking a greater happiness together
than we have known, you whose joy of life, wonder of nature,
appreciation of art and music so exactly match my own.

I received a postcard from you just at the moment I felt
most apprehensive, thinking you might have forgotten me,
not wanting to admit, even to myself, how greatly your
absence had affected me, re-read your words several times
looking for some deeper meaning behind the straightforward
information it contained:

'Hello there. Progress slow. I spent one whole day in Rome area.
Have learnt that the plan is changed and shall be returning to UK
after New Delhi. EA plans in abeyance. Possibly cancelled
altogether. Must wait and see.'

Betty Mealand

Why Me?

Cushioned, lulled gently, to and fro.
A tiny seed planted, continues to grow.
Despite all hardships, many problems, and strife.
Cocooned in its chrysalis, pure waters of life.
Nurtured constantly, by life force within
With strong, pulsating life-line.
So much warmth, and nourishment here,
What could there be, to cause any fear?
Yet there is a deep ache, within the soul,
Will I rest here, until I am whole?
Still, no answer, to my plaintive cry
Only vague misgivings, such a deep deep sigh.
There is passage of time, the great race.
By now, more growth, has taken place.
Tiny hands move, stretch out
A feeling of wanting to be out
Yet one listens to the soul, as always.
Content to wait, these nights, and days.
Until sharp point, of piercing lance.
Like him, I do not stand a chance.
Bathed in crimson life-blood.
Which falls as gentle rain,
Who will say, I died in vain?

Terri Fisher

Wedded Bliss

I can only view life a woman's way
As I cope with the children and the chores each day.
Wondering how far the money will go
And how long before John's shoes let in the snow.

The baby keeps crying, but smiles when I'm seen
Was the wedded bliss, just a utopian dream
Has our young love got lost in the maze
As peeling potatoes out the window I gaze.

Seated round the table are my love and my life,
Did you visage the struggle when I became your wife.
I look at your dear face, head bent over your plate
I wonder had you noticed you hair going grey of late.

How do you see me, I ask myself often,
Are the dreams of our youth, blown away and forgotten,
You raise up your head, your eyes seek my face
You whisper I love you, I'm content with my place.

Wyn Downs

DAUGHTERS OF EVE

Women, women, I am your soul,
Hear me when I cry:
It is your cry.

Dragged from between
Your mother's trembling legs,
The first cry, the last cry,
One and the same.

She screamed for you,
Screamed that you be boy,
Cried that you were not,
Wept in shame.

Taught you how to hide
Your ache for freedom
As she swallowed
Her own mother's pain.

Told you it was worthy
To be mother of sons:
Eve's redemption,
Recreating Adam's name.

Women, don't deny
Your souls, I beg you,
Scream for a girl-child,
Break this chain.

Women, women, I am your soul,
Hear me when I cry:
It is your cry.

Annie Lovelock

FREEDOM

I'm no longer your wife
No longer living in shadows and fear
Free to blossom like a flower
Now I know you're nowhere near

Freedom, I want to see the world twice
Freedom, I want to experience a thousand vice
Just because I'm free
Free of him, just to be me

No sentimental looking back
How can a living nightmare be fun
No tearful regrets of what we might have had
I have my daughter, we'll live it up in the sun.

Freedom, I want to see the world twice
Freedom, I want to experience a thousand vice
Just because I'm free
Free of him, just to be me

I can find *me* at last
No longer his housemaid.
I can find out what *I* like
No longer chained to the sink, afraid
I've no fear, I can be me
Just because I am *free*.

Ann Burgess

Words

After her first stroke
Some words were blurred.

After the second
She babbled as she dribbled.

They brought a board, to point with the wasting hand.

Food. Drink. Bed. - Pan. Yes. No.

For these were all the words they needed
To meet her needs.

And she had been a poet.

Margaret Bark

Why

It seemed, when he was four years old,
That not a day went by
Without his tugging at my hand
And asking, 'Why, mum . . . why?
Why must we wipe shoes on the mat?
Why is that lady very fat?
And why can't Santa bring a cat?
Please tell me why, Mum . . . why?'

A few years later, now at school,
He still would question why.
Sometimes I found it very hard
An answer to supply.
'Why can't we count the stars at night?
Why can't jets go as fast as light?
Why do some countries want to fight?'
He asked me. 'Why, Mum . . . why?'

He didn't ask me much at all
Over the past few years . . .
A teenage lad won't go to Mum
To tell his dreams and fears.
Now questions rack and torture me . . .
'Why couldn't you the dangers see?
Why did you take the Ecstasy?
Why *you*, love?
            Why, son . . . why?'

Christine Matthews

THE LUGGAGE OF LIFE

Still boxed in the bottom of my wardrobe are the shoes
From my heyday, winkle-pickers with pointed toes,
Gold sandals with stiletto heels. I loved the fashionable frou-frous
Of circular skirts, petticoats in net, paper nylon or broderie anglaise
which shows
Beneath a pretty frill. Now I look at my feet
And feel like an ugly sister. Forty years on
Those dainty shoes no longer fit. My pace is not as fleet.
I think of time spent on elaborate hairstyles, all the pins in my chignon.
I would pack my case with an assortment of bikinis
And head for the French Riviera. I scoured the shops
For unusual earrings, rode to pop concerts in taxis,
Watched the fountain of perfume fall in scented drops.
I buttoned cummerbunds round my slender waist
And draped stoles round my tanned shoulders.
My cousin to shatter the glamour showed his distaste.
'Your green eyeshadow makes you look like a crocodile in muddy
waters'
Forgiving I joined him and his footballer friends
Even if I wasn't enthusiastic about the game.
He took me to a firework display to make amends
And to a restaurant where the chef ignited the brandy. The flame
Reflected in the silver dish smouldered and died
And so did my youth forever gone but not forgotten.
Now I prefer the comfort of my own fireside,
Winter evenings occupied with needle, book and pen.
Instead of green eyelids I cultivate green fingers
Spending Summer days tending plants to attract butterfly and bee,
Pampering my pussy and listening to her purrs,
Experiencing joy and sorrow, observing happiness and tragedy.
Old age seemed an eternity away, an inevitability on a distant horizon
Already I am on the threshold carrying a suitcase of memories
treasured and golden.

Vivienne Brocklehurst

SCORPIO RISING

Some women are dangerous.
These are the women who ride dragons.
They defy all and become one.

Loving man and women.

Born of blood and filled with fire.
Some women are bathed in light,
for strength they take the lightning and weave it into anger.

She will rise before us,
this woman born of fire.

They walk on the edge of the cloud
holding the lightning and the thunder.

The wind may fill their senses.
But the world has drained their hearts.
Women that belong to no-one
but themselves, blind faith and destiny.

She smells of crushed herbs and summer light.
Clothed in lilac mist.

Unchanging as the mountains yet fickle as the tide.
These women care far more than the strong are supposed to.

Defying the laws of old and building a new era of hope.

For these are the strong, not the weak.
The survivors, no longer the defeated victims.

Fiery passion and unearthly calm.

These are the women of reckoning.
Some sit by the fire,
others dance in the flames.

Fleur Panis

YOURSELF

The most special person in your life
Is the one you should understand.
Your heart should be given to yourself
Before you share it with someone else.
Take a little time out to know your mind
What's really going on inside.
Look into your heart, see what's there
Who you want to be tender and care.
Who you need around, day in and day out
Should also be found out.
Give yourself a little time to work things through
That extra moment can be so important to you.

Karen Gorman

PILLS

Pills, you try to tempt me, urging me to take
An overdose to oblivion, from which I'd never wake
Life is full of upset, no longer can I cope
What's the point of living, when I only want to mope?

Jilted by my boyfriend, whom I thought was ever true
Until he told me it was over, our relationship was through
I cannot live without him, nor do I want to try
Should I take you pills, and lay down here to die?

No, pills, you're not the answer - I have to face the pain
The hurt and dented ego and learn to live again
He wasn't all that perfect, clear I now can see
Blinded by my love, was I, he's not the man for me!

At 16, I should not despair, there's better men than him
My first lost love now fading, no need to be so grim!
I'll find, in time, my true love, some day he'll come along
So, pills, you cannot tempt me, my zest for life is strong!

Mary Wood

DANGEROUS LOVE

Bars surround me
Jailed for life
Forcing me to like

He tells me I am beautiful
He asks me for a hug
'No,' I tell him
But he hears only what he wants

Everywhere I look
He . . . is there
Watching me
Staring at me

He fancies me
He flatters me
He follows me

He wants to be with me

He makes me feel lonely
He makes me feel confused
He makes me feel special
And he makes me feel used.

H A M

THIS WOMAN OF THE WORLD

I'm a woman of the world - I rise at six,
I poke the fire, I get the coal, and put on sticks.
I'm a woman of the world, I go to bed at one,
But just before I go - I make sure all the jobs are done.
I'm a woman of the world - I know my worth,
I was in on Women's Lib right from its birth.
I'm a woman of the world - I know my place,
I leave just five minutes to do my hair and face.
I'm a woman of the world - I'm on a diet,
I swim at lunchtimes, and enjoy the peace and quiet.
I'm a woman of the world, the arts and crafts are my great love,
And I write poems - getting inspiration from above.
I'm a woman of the world - and you could say,
That I fill up every minute of every waking day.
I'm a woman of the world, but I get very tired,
- It's hard to be so wonderful and stay inspired.
I'm a woman of the world, and I can do just anything,
I can run and I can dance, I can laugh and I can sing.
I've learnt to re-assess myself, and walk amidst the dew,
On an early morning when I leave the sleeping you.
I've learnt to be alternative, not let them grind me down,
And externally I'm smiling,
But inside there's just a hint of frown.

I'm a woman of the world but you can see,
That there are many facets that go to make up me . . .

Jane Mills

TOUCHED

You touched me

telling me about the night you,
contemplating stopping before starting
awoke to feel me touching you and changed your mind

you touched me

holding my head like Hamlet,
suddenly quiet in the centre of sweating flight,
when the words 'you're so precious to me' fell like snow

you touched me

with slow tears seeping from a burning house of picture past
trying to quench the cold-hot fears of bodies left behind
no-one but you could save

you touched me

held me

but you could not hold on to me.

Feather softness turned to grasping, pinching, slapping
the duststorms of your scratching needs lodged in my lungs
damped only by the saddest salt that falls there now and where

you touched me.

Janet Kersey

EQUAL STATUS

Men and women who toiled tirelessly in their day.
Recompensed for long hours, with a meagre wage.
Those days were tough and pretty rough, all work no play.
Those folk have reached the time, some termed Brave Age.

Honesty and trustworthiness was a priority in their time.
Armed with Christian Faith, to others they proved kind.
Bringing up a family on a meagre wage no waste very hard.
True stalwarts of our country, they sure played a part.

Travelling to work, cycling or walking for a mile or two.
Continued to their work destination by bus taxi or train.
Parents keeping the home together their priority and aim.
Few broken marriages then, and crime much less too.

To worship on Sundays for the family complete was a must.
Daily prayers undertaken, praying to God in whom they trust.
Respecting the tradition of others was what they believed.
Their neighbour's need was a commitment they did meet.

A stable family life living for each other was their goal.
No money to spare for non necessities, squandering none.
The family reminiscence their tender years and Oh what fun.
And the advancement of years when they had to share the workload.

Alas in adolescence, an occupation of choice,so off they went.
Their parents relax and save a few pounds, not on luxury spent.
For they worked tirelessly and for a living they strived.
In their latter years, paying for care, Oh, what a sorry plight.

Women understand the cost of residential care, they can demand.
For a quality of life, not quantity for the elderly in the land.
All is wanted is equal status, with those who do not have to pay.
Those who saved, entitlement to reside free at the end of the day.

Elizabeth Swaile

How I Feel When He Doesn't Phone

Stomach on fire, fists clenched,
Nails in palms, heart wrenched.
Furrowed brow, tense jaw,
Eyes blazing, cheeks red raw.
Body slumped, back bent,
Shoulders down, feeling pent.
Can't rest, I'll do my best.
Relax a little, body's brittle.
My hearing like radars, unhealed scars.
Don't like feeling this way, go away.
Self-esteem has hit rock bottom, the feelings not forgotten.
Rejected.
Dejected.
Unselected.
Unprotected.
I stand corrected, he's the same as every other.
He's just another.
He's just an other.

Hannah Mew

A Woman Scorned

Mother Nature is vexed, she can see no mirth
in occurrences since her explicit induction.
For man has defiled and abused the earth
bringing evil, plaque and corruption.
Then technology evolved and, along with its birth
came environmental and social destruction.

Pollution is rampant in soil, sea and air
from toxic chemicals (which mankind have designed).
And the humans themselves, from perverted repair
are unclean, in both body and mind.
But with the ultimate insult - her impaired ozone layer,
Mother Nature will not long remain blind

to the intolerable tampering - the vile intervention
of the cycle of life, death and rebirth.
To organs transplanted from animal to human
while uprooting the lungs of the earth.
And worse is the fatally pemature plan
to explore the vast, obscure girth

of the universe - we were never intended
to meddle with cosmic rules, strictly attended.
So beware! Her benevolence will one day be amended
and the efforts of wicked humans suspended . . .
. . . then a silence, profane and profound be descended
. . . when Mother Nature's dire wrath is finally ended!

Sylvia Wright

PASSING TIME

It's odd to look inside the mirror and see a stranger's face.
It can't be me there looking back, the years have flown a frightening pace.
Surely this must be another, for I am older than my mother.
I lost her many years ago, when I was only young,
And life's been a harsh and lonely ride without her there and by my side.
In my heart has always been despair, there was always something missing there.
It's something time can never heal, something wrong - something real.
Oh, there's been so many times, I've needed her to be
A rock, a friend and even foe, and just be there for me.
And through the years, through young and old
These times have built - too many to be told.
I needed her when I began to grow, from childhood into things I didn't know.
Things I had to face alone, things I needed to be shown.
She missed my marriage - and divorce, and the hell that came between,
And if she'd been there with her view, perhaps I might have missed them too.
One event in my life, I needed her so much,
And going through a lot of strife, I longed for mother's touch,
But she wasn't there, I had to bear the fact that she was gone.
I missed her strength and mother's comfort.
She - missed the birth of her grandson.
The happy times are not so few, but she can never share them too,
And the joy can never fill the part, of that emptiness within my heart.
Now age has begun to unfold, I need her once again,
I need to know the facts of life, of beginning to grow old.
I need her there for nurture and comfort, I want to sit upon her knee.
I want to feel and hold the long lost love, I know she held for me.
I need her wise and knowing ways, I need her love, I need her praise.
I need her guidance that can come from no other,
Even though - I'm older than my mother.

C Neale-Eyre

FOOD FOR THOUGHT

Mirror, mirror on the wall,
You cause me great disquiet.
The theme is always the same,
Diet! Diet! Diet!

Oh dear! I like my food,
Fish and chips and peas,
Followed by a nice ice-cream,
Or crackers wine and cheese.

I really must fight the urge,
And control the bulges,
For every bit of extra food,
Eventually divulges.

Eugenie Barker

Emotional Riot

Blood pours out of wounds, ripped apart by words of hate,
I sink to my knees and cover my eyes
I've been dreaming of this of late.

Why do I feel the way I do? I cry and wring my hands - feel so alone,
When all around me are people - laughing, dancing, singing,
Words of love.

Why mock my emotions? Pretend they are just a farce.
I weep, shout and hurl - emotional bricks at myself.

Wendy Cain

Steam Trains

Why does the sight of a steam locomotive
Turn all those grown men into small boys
All excited at the plume of steam bellowing from
A dirty noisy engine emitting shrieks to wake the dead
They all flock to see and photograph
And talk of the engine as if a woman
She this and she that is all the conversation
When anyone can see that this monstrosity
Must be male with the coaxing noises used to start it off
The huge shovelful of coals no female would swallow
The noise of the wheels on the track
They polish and buff away at the iron horse
With oily rags no decent woman would own
What pleasure exudes from them all
The dirty faces beaming in the light
Grime-encrusted hands holding mugs of tea
As they talk of their day and duties
This steam engine to them is alive
Part of their heritage as it hared across the countryside
I can see the power in iron horse
I know the independence given to the travellers
But a woman inside this noisy locomotive
No no - all male power there

Joan Smith

PART-TIME DAD

The little boy waits for the knock on the door,
He wants to tell daddy his hand is sore,
Sadly it happened a week ago,
It was then he wanted his daddy to know.

Now at school he still waits for his dad,
He wants to tell him school's not bad,
But it's not the week for his dad to come,
'Will it be soon?' he asked his mum.

Now the boy is eleven years old,
The visits are now once a month he is told,
He's working hard and in the top stream,
If only dad knew he was in the football team.

He's now a young man and soon leaving school,
And he's passed his exams and proved he's no fool,
His dad wasn't there when he got his degree,
There was so much his dad didn't see.

But spare a thought for the dad who's not there,
It's easy to think he just doesn't care,
He didn't plan to be a part-time dad,
The system dictated when he would see his lad.

Now a man with a mind of his own,
He now knows things he had never known,
How his dad regrets not always being there,
And how life sadly is sometimes not fair.

The father now waits for the knock on the door,
And he urges his son to always be sure,
He wanted things to be different for his lad,
For it's no fun at all being a part-time dad.

Celia Law

THERAPY

The territory of wild heart is beating;
beating with anger, beating with shame.
Sorrow like rocks, solid as boulders
sit so weighty upon her small shoulders.

'Will I end up in the loony bin?' she laughs,
on the edge of life, on the rim
of a beckoning pit.

And there she sits,
just calling her memories in.

She will find a safe ledge to examine her terror,
find herself in the dusty mirror.

No longer is she the friend or the worker,
no longer the failure, the heartbroken lover,
no longer the person or people who knew her.
Just finding herself in the dusty mirror.

And eventually the stone becomes wood,
it burns into ash then turns into water.
She feels the touch of a gentle healer,
a voice deep within which makes not a sound,
the shadow becoming the person she's found.

And the ghosts make their way
to a different past.

Janice Murga

A Dog Talking

I'm at an animal rescue centre
Waiting for a home.
My other owners abandoned me
And left me free to roam.
They got me for Christmas
For the kids to love and adore
A sweet puppy, six weeks old
Who could ask for more?
But I needed walking
And of course I grew and grew
They grew out of love with me
Which made me sad and blue.
So I'm waiting for a family
Who will treat me very kind
And realise a dog's for life
And not just for Christmas time.

Jenny Bosworth

Aerobics!

Oh dear! Not that day again!
Are you ready for all the pain?
Don trainers, leotard, to cavort
Crucifying muscles, given for support
Join the line of bodies, waiting to begin
The heaving, straining, to music that's 'in'
Perspiring and tiring, but daren't drop out
Or the steely eyed instructor will shout
His rippling muscles, are envied near and far
But it's his living, kidding, you'll be a star
He doesn't care about your aching back
Or feeling like Guy Fawkes on the rack
This costly routine, now considered a craft
Used to be achieved, with a hard day's graft!

Mabel Wall

Mother

I was very young
She washed and dressed me.
I wouldn't eat my meals
Mother grew angry.

I cried at bedtime,
Didn't want to leave them together
By a cosy fireside
I alone upstairs.

I was naughty when friends called
Enjoyed embarrassing her.
She should be playing with *me*
I sulk.

I told tales to daddy, half lies
There was a row daddy left us
I sobbed but mother loved me
She promised *she* would never leave me
I slept smugly.

She is very old
I wash and dress her
She picks at her food
I'm so angry.

Won't ever go to bed early
Never leaves my lover and I alone
By the fireside
To talk, to love, to be together.

It's worse when friends visit
Makes rude comments
Worse when she won't talk
Old, hunched, forbidding
Reminding us of our fate.

She lied to my lover about me
He left and she wept bitterly at my tears
I hold her in my arms rocking her
Promising to look after her always
Inside my head I'm screaming
Will it never end.

Virginia Games

God Make Me

God made me a woman
with all my faculty
and so I must be.
With eyes to see the need of others,
with ears to hear the cry of children
with nose to smell the stench of sin
womb to bring forth child. Breasts to give them suck
and hands to care, to nurse, to cherish, and embrace
and give to those in need.
Feet to stand upright in the raging storm
and life, that I may live forever.

God made me a woman,
and that's just what I want to be
I am one of His unique creation
His beauty in me I see
There must be a special reason
why He chose to let me be,
a woman with all my faculty.

Whistel Edwards-Arnold

A Woman's Work

A woman's work is never done
No matter what they say
I have tried to get my husband to help me around the house
But he won't help me no way.

A woman's work is never done
Even when I lived at home
For when my father got home from work
He just used to sit there and moan.

A woman's work is never done
I have to plan and think ahead
The only time I will find some rest
Is really when I am dead.

Keith L Powell

Girls Without Fathers Are Looking For Love

For some time now
we've been disliked
for our long eyes and what we see, we see.
We're hoping this won't put you off
For we are loving
and we aim to please.

We only look for good in people
And we know you have a sense of humour.
We'll mimic you,
You'll like it.

Also we are sure that you have pain
which we can heal with our ways
For sure we are loving
And we aim to please.

Sarah Thompson

Nihil Obstat

(there is no obstacle)

Somniferous waves lapped and rolled
overlooking Irish Sea. Fair child's innocence
rested upon tempestuous breakers. Rippling,
rolling inner thoughts. Cascading energy
encouraged mild accomplishment, though
role and righteousness tore suppressed heart,
beat into guilt of one's slaughter. All
family beliefs collided with verisimilitude.
Pulverise that non-existent memory.

nemo me impune lacissit
(no one hurts me with impunity)

Forgive a creation endangered by travelling
smuggler off-loading one future beat?
Society decide . . . foetus float to peace,
away from complication of orders.

Russell Cross

INFORMATION

We hope you have enjoyed reading this book - and that you will continue to enjoy it in the coming years.

If you like reading and writing poetry drop us a line, or give us a call, and we'll send you a free information pack.

Write to :-

WomensWords Information
1-2 Wainman Road
Woodston
Peterborough
PE2 7BU
(01733) 230746